I CHOOSE

31 Day Devotional

Precious Mast

For
INITIATIVE

Copyright © 2020 Precious Mast

All rights reserved

No part of this book may be reproduced, or stored in a retrieval system, or transmitted in any form or by any means, electronic, mechanical, photocopying, recording, or otherwise, without express written permission of the publisher.

ISBN: 9798583591800

Printed in the United States of America

CONTENTS

Title Page

Copyright

Introduction

1. Wisdom   1

2. Forgiveness   3

3. Humility   5

4. Joy   7

5. Worship   9

6. Confidence   11

7. Hope   13

8. Prayer   15

9. Love   17

10. Obedience   19

11. Holiness   21

12. Patience   23

13. Contentment   25

14. Confession   27

15. Faithfulness   29

16. Serving   31

17. Encouragement   33

18. Goodness   35

19. Freedom	37
20. Listening	39
21. Light	41
22. Grace	43
23. Purpose	45
24. Victory	47
25. Peace	49
26. Kindness	51
27. Abiding	53
28. Honor	55
29. Thankfulness	57
30. Growth	59
31. Faith	61
Notes	63
About The Author	65

INTRODUCTION

Every day you have choices to make in life. The choice to get out of bed, what you will eat, if you're going to exercise, what you will wear, what time you will leave for work, etc. But you also have choices when it comes to your spiritual life.

In the spring of 2019, God led my family to take a step of faith out of our comfort zone (West Virginia) and move to a new state (Michigan) for a new job for my husband. That alone caused all kinds of emotions for me in the first few months of living here. I struggled with looking back at where we came from. Many of those first few weeks would find me on walks, sometimes talking out loud to God wondering what He was doing. Yet thru all of that doubting and wondering on my end, there was the still small voice of the Holy Spirit asking me if I trusted Him. Did I trust that He knew what He was doing? I had a choice to make right then and there. Would I allow my emotions to get in the way of God's plan for my life and all He wanted to teach me? Or would I choose to surrender. And so it began, the choices I had to make each day in my spiritual life so that I could fully live the abundant life He had for me in Jesus.

As time went on, these God honoring choices I had to make became so real to me because they would help set the tone for my day. Random thoughts would come to mind from my devotional time regarding choices and I would mention the idea of a small devotional book about this to a few people in my life. When I did, each one would tell me they would enjoy reading something along those lines with a challenge each day.

I started compiling scripture in a folder but then decided it wouldn't amount to much so I ignored it. The problem, was that I kept facing these choices every day in my life and realized they weren't going away. How was I going to respond? I thought about the idea of creating a devotional but then decided it was too much work, so I ignored it. Then fall came and life slowed down a bit and my husband encouraged me to take some time to write.

This 31 day devotional is a simple reminder of the choices you have been given. I challenge you to set aside 5 minutes and read one each day as you strive to live out that choice with the help of the Holy Spirit. You will notice that word being played out in multiple ways thru your day if you allow it. Each day as you read truth from God's Word, let it soak in and saturate all that you are. It is then that you will be able to make these God honoring choices. My desire is for you to see more of who Jesus is as you strive to imitate Him.

"He must become greater; I must become less." John 3:30 (NIV)

1. WISDOM

"For the Lord gives wisdom; from His mouth come knowledge and understanding." Proverbs 2:6 (NIV)

"If any of you lacks wisdom, you should ask God, who gives generously to all without finding fault, and it will be given to you. But when you ask, you must believe and not doubt, because the one who doubts is like a wave of the sea, blown and tossed by the wind. That person should not expect to receive anything from the Lord." James 1:5 (NIV)

✳ ✳ ✳

Wisdom: *the quality of having experience, knowledge, and good judgment; the quality of being wise.*

How often do you find yourself longing to make wise decisions throughout your day, yet forget where true wisdom comes from? Wisdom is found in God Himself. Humbling yourself before Him and spending time in His presence is what makes you wise.

When God told King Solomon in 1 Kings 3 he could ask for one request, he chose wisdom. He could have asked for wealth, long life or the life of his enemies, but that was all secondary for Solomon because he knew that in order to oversee the kingdom of Israel in a God honoring way, he would need wisdom. God was so pleased with Solomon's request that He gave him wisdom along with what he didn't ask for as well.

Humbly ask God for wisdom today, but remember what James says, when you ask for it, you must believe and not doubt.

Practice The Word:
Ask God for WISDOM today.

Study Deeper:
King Solomon in 1&2 Kings and the book of Proverbs.

2. FORGIVENESS

"For if you forgive other people when they sin against you, your heavenly Father will also forgive you. But if you do not forgive others their sins, your Father will not forgive your sins." Matthew 6:14-15 (NIV)

"Bear with each other and forgive one another if any of you has a grievance against someone. Forgive as the Lord forgave you." Colossians 3:13 (NIV)

❋ ❋ ❋

Forgiveness: *the action or process of forgiving or being forgiven.*

Forgiveness. Sometimes this word can be a hard pill to swallow, especially if someone has hurt you deeply and left you with unforgettable wounds.

On the other hand, the beauty of this word is that when you apply it and choose to offer it, you see Jesus for who He is in your own life. He chose to go to the cross and die, giving His life to offer you forgiveness when you did not deserve it.

Forgiveness is the only thing that can bring you freedom in this life. First you need to accept it from Jesus Himself for your sin and then offer it to someone who has hurt you.

Practice The Word:
Who do you need to FORGIVE today?

Study Deeper:
Matthew 6:1-15.

3. HUMILITY

"Do nothing out of selfish ambition or vain conceit. Rather, in humility value others above yourselves, not looking to your own interests but each of you to the interests of the others." Philippians 2:3-4 (NIV)

"When pride comes, then comes disgrace, but with humility comes wisdom." Proverbs 11:2 (NIV)

"He has told you, O man, what is good; and what does the Lord require of you, but to do justice, to love kindness, and to walk humbly with your God?" Micah 6:8 (NASB)

❉ ❉ ❉

Humility: *a modest or low view of one's own importance; humbleness.*

Why is humility such an important quality? The opposite of humility is pride and scripture tells us from James 4:6, that *"God opposes the proud, but gives grace to the humble,"* and then in verse 10, *"Humble yourselves in the presence of the Lord, and He will exalt you."*

When I think back to Joshua in the Old Testament I see a man who humbly served in the background as Moses' servant. After Moses died, God puts Joshua as the leader of Israel. Joshua walked humbly with

God, being careful to observe His commands and because of that we see God exalting him. Joshua 3:7, *"Now the Lord said to Joshua, 'This day I will begin to exalt you in the sight of all Israel, that they may know that just as I have been with Moses, I will be with you,'"* and then in 4:14, *"On that day the Lord exalted Joshua in the sight of all Israel."*

Humility is not an easy quality to choose. You will notice pride trying to creep its way into any area of your life possible, but that does not mean you don't fight against it. With the Holy Spirit's help, you can wage war against pride and overcome it with humility, knowing that if you choose it, God will exalt you in His time.

Practice The Word:
How can you practice HUMILITY today?

Study Deeper:
Philippians 2:1-11, James 4:1-10, Colossians 3:12-17 & 1 Peter 5:5b-6.

4. JOY

"Rejoice always, pray continually, give thanks in all circumstances; for this is God's will for you in Christ Jesus." 1 Thessalonians 5:16-18 (NIV)

❊ ❊ ❊

Joy: *"Joy is the settled assurance that God is in control of all the details of my life, the quiet confidence that ultimately everything is going to be all right, and the determined choice to praise God in all things." (Warren)*

This most glorious word can be one of difficulty to choose most days. You are often told that Joy = Happiness, but that is far from the truth. You don't have to feel happy to have joy.

I remember often as a child finding myself in situations that I did not like or were not making me happy. My sweet Mom would come to me more than I can remember and ask me the question, *"Precious, are you choosing joy?"* Joy was the last thing that I wanted to choose, but to this day, my Mom taught me something that I will forever cherish and that is, no matter how or what I am feeling in a situation I always have the opportunity to honor my Savior and choose joy.

For me, joy is knowing that all is well because God is in control. All He asks of me is to faithfully, humbly and quietly walk thru this life with Him and enJOY His presence. True joy is only found in Jesus and leads you to praise Him.

Practice The Word:
How can you choose JOY today?

Study Deeper:
Philippians 4 & Romans 12:9-21.

5. WORSHIP

"Lord, you are my God; I will exalt you and praise your name, for in perfect faithfulness you have done wonderful things, things planned long ago." Isaiah 25:1 (NIV)

"God is spirit, and his worshipers must worship in the Spirit and in truth." John 4:24 (NIV)

❋ ❋ ❋

Worship: *Biblical worship is the full-life response- head, heart, and hands- to who God is and what He has done.*

I consider myself blessed to be married to the greatest worshipper I know, my husband, who happens to be a Worship Pastor. He has taught me so much about what true worship looks like. You can make great music, but if your heart is not in the right place it means nothing to God.

King David is probably known as the greatest worshipper of all time. He wrote the majority of the Psalms you read and even sing today. Take a look at the specific instructions given in John 4:24 to worship in Spirit AND truth. Often it is easy to think worship just involves music, but the truth of God's word is of equal or greater value to how you worship.

Know this, you were created to worship and scripture says in Luke 19:40 that if you remain silent, then the rocks will cry out in worship of Him. Charles Spurgeon wrote,

"If I did not praise and bless Christ my Lord, I should deserve to have my tongue torn out by its roots from my mouth. If I did not bless and magnify his name, I should deserve that every stone I tread on in the streets should rise up to curse my ingratitude, for I am a drowned debtor to the mercy of God – over head and ears – to infinite love and boundless compassion I am a debtor. Are you not the same? Then I charge you by the love of Christ, awake, awake your hearts now to magnify his glorious name."

Practice The Word:
What does true WORSHIP look like for you today?

Study Deeper:
1 Chronicles 29:10-20, Psalm 34.

6. CONFIDENCE

"But blessed is the one who trusts in the LORD, whose confidence is in him." Jeremiah 17:7 (NIV)

"Therefore, since we have a great high priest who has ascended into heaven, Jesus the Son of God, let us hold firmly to the faith we profess. For we do not have a high priest who is unable to empathize with our weaknesses, but we have one who has been tempted in every way, just as we are—yet he did not sin. Let us then approach God's throne of grace with confidence, so that we may receive mercy and find grace to help us in our time of need." Hebrews 4:14-16 (NIV)

* * *

Confidence: *the feeling or belief that one can rely on someone or something; firm trust.*

When I talk about confidence here I am not meaning confidence that comes from you. The only reason you are able to exude confidence is because of the work of Jesus in your life. Confidence comes from Him.

Did you notice that grace and mercy are mentioned at the very end of Hebrews 4:16? I believe that in order to have a God honoring confidence, grace and mercy must be seen within you as well, just like Jesus exemplified while on this earth.

There is no need for you to shrink back and be timid when it comes to your faith. Jesus calls you to step out in bold, confident faith to share His gospel with others. One of the most confident but humble men, Paul, said in Romans 1:16,

"For I am not ashamed of the gospel, because it is the power of God that brings salvation to everyone who believes: first to the Jew, then to the Gentile."

Practice The Word:
What is holding you back from being CONFIDENT and sharing your faith today?

Study Deeper:
Proverbs 14:26, 1 John 5:13-15, 2 Corinthians 3.

7. HOPE

"Praise be to the God and Father of our Lord Jesus Christ! In his great mercy he has given us new birth into a living hope through the resurrection of Jesus Christ from the dead, and into an inheritance that can never perish, spoil or fade. This inheritance is kept in heaven for you." 1 Peter 1:3-4 (NIV)

"For in this hope we were saved. But hope that is seen is no hope at all. Who hopes for what they already have? But if we hope for what we do not yet have, we wait for it patiently." Romans 8:24 (NIV)

❈ ❈ ❈

Hope: *a feeling of expectation and desire for a certain thing to happen, a feeling of trust.*

It is easy to place your hope in many things, ie. the government, humanity, finances, employers, sports teams, relationships and yet all of these can fail you. There is only one place to put your Hope that will never fail and that is in Jesus Christ.

Putting your hope and trust in Jesus will secure your eternity and bring about the real peace you are longing for. What does it require of you? Patience. Your Living Hope, Jesus, will be revealed in God's perfect timing.

Practice The Word:
What are you placing your HOPE in today?

Study Deeper:
1 Peter 1.

8. PRAYER

"For the eyes of the Lord are on the righteous and his ears are attentive to their prayer, but the face of the Lord is against those who do evil." 1 Peter 3:12 (NIV)

"Be joyful in hope, patient in affliction, faithful in prayer." Romans 12:12 (NIV)

"Devote yourselves to prayer, being watchful and thankful." Colossians 4:2 (NIV)

❊ ❊ ❊

Prayer: *a spiritual communion with God, as in supplication, thanksgiving, adoration, or confession.*

One of the sweetest memories I have in college was my prayer time with the Lord. I remember it well because I experienced an ongoing communication with Him wherever I was, on or off campus. As I walked thru the hallways to and from class, the gym, work, the cafeteria and around Chicago I was often praying silently. The simple fact about prayer is that it is just talking to God.

How often do you find yourself in a day talking to everyone else but God? I know I am guilty of this. I've had times when I was so frustrated with life and would try to call a family member or close friend to talk and every time they would never answer the phone. Eventually I realized it was because God was quietly waiting for me to talk to Him about it.

When God answers your prayers, do you find yourself responding back to Him in praise? He longs to have communion with you in this way. Don't deprive Him of it any longer.

Jesus is your example of what a life of prayer looks like. Luke 5:16 says, *"But Jesus Himself would often slip away to the wilderness and pray."* Did you know Jesus prayed for you before He left this earth? Check out John 17.

Practice The Word:
Set aside 10 minutes to PRAY today?

Study Deeper:
Matthew 6:5-15, John 17 & Philippians 4:6-7.

9. LOVE

"A new command I give you: Love one another. As I have loved you, so you must love one another. By this everyone will know that you are my disciples, if you love one another." John 13:34-35 (NIV)

" Dear children, let us not love with words or speech but with actions and in truth." 1 John 3:18 (NIV)

"We love because He first loved us." 1 John 4:19 (NIV)

❊ ❊ ❊

Love: *"Love is patient, love is kind. It does not envy, it does not boast, it is not proud. It does not dishonor others, it is not self-seeking, it is not easily angered, it keeps no record of wrongs. Love does not delight in evil but rejoices with the truth. It always protects, always trusts, always hopes, always perseveres." 1 Corinthians 13:4-7*

This word is little in size but has the greatest meaning. If you could conquer this one virtue, love, then all the others would fall into place behind it. Why is love so hard to get right? Probably because it requires sacrifice on your end.

When looking at the greatest example of love, you see Jesus who was willing to give and sacrifice His life so you could be forgiven. How far are you willing to go to show love? Jesus said that if you could learn to love as He did (all people, not just the easy ones), that would be your greatest testimony.

Often it is easy to say you love someone, but Jesus reminds us that it is not just saying the words, we have to live them out with actions and in truth.

Practice The Word:
Who do you need to show LOVE to today?

Study Deeper:
1 John & Romans 12:9-21.

10. OBEDIENCE

"Jesus replied, "Anyone who loves me will obey my teaching. My Father will love them, and we will come to them and make our home with them." John 14:23 (NIV)

"Do not merely listen to the word, and so deceive yourselves. Do what it says." James 1:22 (NIV)

❋ ❋ ❋

Obedience: *compliance with an order, request, or law or submission to another's authority.*

This word is hard for all humans to follow. It proves itself by going all the way back to the fall in Genesis 3 when Adam and Eve decided to disobey the one rule God put in place for them. This rule was even to protect them.

Do you believe that God always has your best interest in mind when He asks you to obey Him and His commands? I know too often I find myself doubting. But it doesn't matter what you or I think, we are told to obey. When you do, it shows your love for Him.

As a follower of Jesus, you need to put yourself under Him and submit in full obedience to His authority in your life. That means putting God in first place and knowing you are a distant second.

Be encouraged by the fact that Jesus Himself was obedient and submitted to the will of His Father when He came down to this earth. Jesus is your example.

Practice The Word:
What do you need to be OBEDIENT before the Lord in today?

Study Deeper:
John 14:15-31

11. HOLINESS

"But just as he who called you is holy, so be holy in all you do; for it is written: 'Be holy, because I am holy.'" 1 Peter 1:15-16 (NIV)

✣ ✣ ✣

Holiness: *set-apart.*

When you think about the word holiness, it seems like such a small word, but with a deep meaning. Believers are called to live a life of holiness, being set apart from the world.

In the above verse you see a command to imitate (which is also known as the highest form of flattery.) God commands us to be holy, just as He is holy. This is not totally possible here on this earth, but that doesn't mean you don't strive daily to put it into practice. Consider it an honor to imitate your Savior.

If you are commanded to live a life of holiness (set apart), how do you live that out while living on this sinful earth? Read Jesus' prayer before He left this earth,

"I have given them your word and the world has hated them, for they are not of the world any more than I am of the world. My prayer is not that you take them out

of the world but that you protect them from the evil one. They are not of the world, even as I am not of it. Sanctify them by the truth; your word is truth. As you sent me into the world, I have sent them into the world."
John 17:14-18

Brothers & Sisters, you live this life of holiness by being sanctified in the truth. That truth being, the Word of God.

Practice The Word:
How can you live a life of HOLINESS today?

Study Deeper:
The book of 1 Peter.

12. PATIENCE

"Whoever is patient has great understanding, but one who is quick-tempered displays folly." Proverbs 14:29 (NIV)

"Be completely humble and gentle; be patient, bearing with one another in love." Ephesians 4:2 (NIV)

"My brothers and sisters, count it all joy when you fall into various trials, knowing that the testing of your faith produces patience. But let patience have its perfect work, that you may be perfect and complete, lacking nothing." James 1:2-4 (NKJV)

❋ ❋ ❋

Patience: *the capacity to accept or tolerate delay, trouble, or suffering without getting angry or upset.*

Patience is a virtue. How many times have you heard that in your life? It's true. Patience for me is probably the hardest virtue to practice. The world today does not help either, always looking for ways to give you instant gratification.

You have many opportunities in a day to practice patience. Whether it's with your spouse, children, co-workers, job, family, neighbors, the coffeemaker, the person at the grocery store or even your waitress at the restaurant. It is so important for the believer to learn patience because it too can be a testimony to those around us.

Scripture speaks of the reward for patience in the verses above. If you live out this word you will have great understanding, along with being perfect and complete, lacking nothing. Perhaps the greatest practice of patience is waiting for the second coming of Jesus. What a reward that will be. Your faith will be made sight!

Practice The Word:
Who do you need to be PATIENT with today?

Study Deeper:
Psalm 37:7-11, Psalm 40 & Ephesians 4:1-3.

13. CONTENTMENT

"...for I have learned to be content whatever the circumstances." Philippians 4:11 (NIV)

❈ ❈ ❈

Contentment: *a state of happiness and satisfaction.*

Contentment. Oh to fully live with this mindset. The verse above was written by the Apostle Paul while in prison (most likely in Rome) for sharing the Gospel. He wrote to the believers in Philippi encouraging them to preach the Gospel, imitate Christ and dwell on excellence.

Imagine being Paul in a dark, cold prison in Rome and writing these words, *"I've learned to be content."* Most of you would not be able to say the same if you were in his situation. Think about your life each day. How many times do you find yourself being discontent? Whether it's with your job, your latest tech gadget, the car you drive, the house you live in or the things you own (because our flesh always wants more). What would your life look like if you were fully content?

Contentment won't come easily, but it can be learned just like Paul said. Is Jesus, the Gospel, your salvation all enough to satisfy your longings? It was for Paul.

Practice The Word:
How can you be CONTENT today?

Study Deeper:
The Apostle Paul and the book of Philippians.

14. CONFESSION

"Have mercy on me, O God, according to your unfailing love; according to your great compassion blot out my transgressions." Psalm 51:1 (NIV)

"Then I acknowledged my sin to you and did not cover up my iniquity. I said, 'I will confess my transgressions to the Lord.' And you forgave the guilt of my sin." Psalm 32:5 (NIV)

"If we confess our sins, he is faithful and just and will forgive us our sins and purify us from all unrighteousness." 1 John 1:9 (NIV)

❊ ❊ ❊

Confession: *a formal statement admitting that one is guilty of a crime.*

King David is known to be one of the greatest examples of how real his sin was to him and how genuinely he confessed it to the Lord. After his adultery with Bathsheba recorded in 2 Samuel 11-12, Nathan the prophet was sent by God to call out the sin in David's life.

When someone calls out sin in your life, you can react to it in one of two ways, 1) let it drive you to anger and flip it around to point out their own sin, or 2) let it drive you to your knees before God in humble confession.

King David chose the second option and you can read his beautiful confession in Psalm 51. God called David, a man after His own heart. This was not because David was perfect by any means, he had his own struggles with sin, but he recognized it within his life and let it lead him to full repentance and confession before God.

Practice The Word:
What sin struggle do you need to CONFESS to Jesus today?

Study Deeper:
Psalm 51 & 32.

15. FAITHFULNESS

"My eyes will be on the faithful in the land, that they may dwell with me; the one whose walk is blameless will minister to me." Psalm 101:6 (NIV)

"Trust in the LORD and do good; Dwell in the land and cultivate faithfulness." Psalm 37:3 (NASB)

"Because of the Lord's great love we are not consumed, for his compassions never fail. They are new every morning; great is your faithfulness." Lamentations 3:22-23 (NIV)

❊ ❊ ❊

Faithfulness: *faithfulness is the concept of unfailingly remaining loyal to someone or something, and putting that loyalty into consistent practice regardless of extenuating circumstances.*

The Bible is full of men and women who were known for their faithfulness, but they did not achieve this on their own. They looked to the One who is and always will be faithful. 2 Timothy 2:13 says, *"if we are faithless, He remains faithful, for He cannot disown Himself."* God embodies this word fully.

Faithfulness is an attribute of God you see carried out thru the whole of Scripture, from beginning to end. You have the privilege of modeling Him again in this way.

The goal for all believers when they enter eternity should be to hear these words from Jesus in Matthew 25:21, *"Well done, good and faithful servant! You have been faithful with a few things; I will put you in charge of many things. Come and share your master's happiness!"* Will they be said of you?

Practice The Word:
In what area of your life can you practice more FAITHFULNESS today?

Study Deeper:
Psalm 36:5-9, 89 & 101.

16. SERVING

"But be sure to fear the LORD and serve him faithfully with all your heart; consider what great things he has done for you." 1 Samuel 12:24 (NIV)

"Whoever serves me must follow me; and where I am, my servant also will be. My Father will honor the one who serves me." John 12:26 (NIV)

"Never be lazy, but work hard and serve the Lord enthusiastically." Romans 12:11 (NLT)

✽ ✽ ✽

Serving: *labor of body or of body and mind, performed at the command of a superior, or the pursuance of duty, or for the benefit of another. Service is voluntary or involuntary.*

The people I have admired most in life are those I have seen serving God and others. Serving is not always a glamorous job, but it wasn't meant to be. It is about learning what it means to put others needs before your own and serve them.

That is exactly what Jesus did when He laid aside who He was and took on the form of a servant (Philippians 2:5-11), coming down to this sinful earth to give His life so you could be forgiven.

Think of the last time you went to a restaurant and

the waiter or waitress who served you at your table. They probably brought you what you asked for, and when you were finished with your meal, they cleaned up after you. Not only that, they would have had other duties that included keeping a clean, inviting environment so you would want to go there in the first place. That type of service is done behind the scenes where you can't see it, but you get to benefit from it.

Sometimes your service is not always seen by others, but it is seen by your Father in heaven. Consider it a joy and honor today to serve those around you.

Practice The Word:
Who can you SERVE today?

Study Deeper:
1 Peter 4:10-11 & Matthew 20:20-28.

17. ENCOURAGEMENT

"But encourage one another daily, as long as it is called 'Today,' so that none of you may be hardened by sin's deceitfulness." Hebrews 3:13 (NIV)

❋ ❋ ❋

Encouragement: *the action of giving someone support, confidence, or hope.*

Think of a person in your life that you would consider your greatest encourager? What did that person do or say that made such an impact on your life?

Encouragement is an action that promotes growth in someone's life. Specific to a believer, when one is encouraged, it can keep them living a holy/set apart life. It can reveal gifts given by the Holy Spirit that need to be used within the local church. It can also keep a discouraged believer active in their faith. It can help someone refocus.

Encouragement is all about coming alongside someone and cheering them on even when they may feel like giving up. You have the opportunity to live this out daily.

Think back again to that great encourager in your life. They helped cheer you on and give you the boost of confidence to be who you are and where you are today. Take some time today to thank them.

Practice The Word:
Who can you ENCOURAGE today?

Study Deeper:
The book of Hebrews & 1 Thessalonians 5.

18. GOODNESS

"Therefore, as we have opportunity, let us do good to all people, especially to those who belong to the family of believers." Galatians 6:10 (NIV)

"For this very reason, make every effort to add to your faith goodness; and to goodness, knowledge; and to knowledge, self-control; and to self-control, perseverance; and to perseverance, godliness; and to godliness, mutual affection; and to mutual affection, love." 2 Peter 1:5-7 (NIV)

❋ ❋ ❋

Goodness: *goodness is a true commitment to choosing right over wrong, good over evil.*

Goodness is found in looking at who God is. This is one of His attributes. All you have to do is look around you to see His goodness on display. Remember His words back in Genesis 1:31 after He created the world? *"God saw all that He had made, and behold, it was very good."* No evil or wrong existed in the beginning.

Goodness is a virtue that God expects to be lived out in the life of a believer. After all it is one of the fruits of the Spirit, and when you choose to live it, you are imitating God in this way.

Throughout the storyline of the Bible, you can see God's goodness displayed over and over again to His people, even when they didn't deserve it. It's not up to you to choose who you show His goodness to, you are just asked to do it. It is a daily commitment that you make with the Holy Spirit's help.

Practice The Word:
How can you show GOODNESS today?

Study Deeper:
Psalm 34:14, 37:3, Titus 2:11-14

19. FREEDOM

"It is for freedom that Christ has set us free. Stand firm, then, and do not let yourselves be burdened again by a yoke of slavery." Galatians 5:1 (NIV)

❋ ❋ ❋

Freedom: *the state of not being imprisoned or enslaved.*

The gift of freedom should never be forgotten. Brothers and sisters, Christ set you free from your slavery to sin! Yet why is it so easy to slide back into sin and feel entangled and burdened with it?

When you think about freedom, often wars and battles come to mind. When a soldier is enlisted and trained for battle, he is taught to stand firm. For the believer, in order to stand firm, there has to be time spent daily being sanctified by the truth of God's Word.

You have been given the Armor of God specifically to fight against the devil and all the fiery darts of sin he will throw at you. The Bible says in Ephesians 6:10-17 to *stand firm* 3 times. Don't let those fiery darts of sin creep in and confuse you.

Jesus waged war to pay for your freedom on the cross. JESUS HAS SET YOU FREE! All He asks of you is to stand firm and live in that freedom.

Practice The Word:
How can you live with Christ's FREEDOM in mind today?

Study Deeper:
Galatians 5 & Ephesians 6:10-17.

20. LISTENING

"There is a time for everything, and a season for every activity under the heavens: ... a time to be silent and a time to speak." Ecclesiastes 3:1 & 7b (NIV)

"Guard your steps when you go to the house of God. Go near to listen rather than to offer the sacrifice of fools, who do not know that they do wrong. Do not be quick with your mouth, do not be hasty in your heart to utter anything before God. God is in heaven and you are on earth, so let your words be few." Ecclesiastes 5:1-2 (NIV)

"My dear brothers and sisters, take note of this: Everyone should be quick to listen, slow to speak and slow to become angry." James 1:19 (NIV)

✼ ✼ ✼

Listening: *give one's attention to a sound, make an effort to hear something; be alert and ready to hear something.*

Listening is something I often struggle with. I want to give my advice or opinion on a matter, or I have a great story to tell. I have to make a conscience effort daily to listen. Distractions by that little device in my hand or even the TV do not help me listen well to my husband, kids and most importantly, God.

Scripture speaks the importance of learning this word and putting it into practice, even when it comes to your time with the Lord. God longs to speak to you, but He's waiting for you to listen.

What would it look like for you to be quiet before God? Psalm 46:10 is a reminder of this. *"Be still, and know that I am God; I will be exalted among the nations, I will be exalted in the earth."*

Practice The Word:
In what way do you need to practice LISTENING today?

Study Deeper:
Ecclesiastes 3:1-11, 5:1-7, Proverbs 17:27-28.

21. LIGHT

"Again Jesus spoke to them, saying, 'I am the light of the world. Whoever follows me will not walk in darkness, but will have the light of life.'" John 8:12 (ESV)

"For you were once darkness, but now you are light in the Lord. Live as children of light." Ephesians 5:8 (NIV)

"Let your light shine before men in such a way that they may see your good works, and glorify your Father who is in heaven." Matthew 5:16 (NASB)

✸ ✸ ✸

Light: *stimulates sight and makes things visible.*

My child recently asked me what God looks like? I had to stop and think for a moment, and then I remembered that several times in Scripture God revealed Himself to people thru a great light. His glory was so radiant that not even the Israelites in the Old Testament could stand to be in the temple.

Light is a glorious thing as it exposes darkness. As a child of God, you are not of the darkness any longer. The darkness of your sin was holding you captive, but as God's child you are no longer bound and are told to, walk as a child of the light. Leave your old, sinful ways behind you.

Who is the light? Scripture tells that Jesus is the

Light of the world. You are to shine Him to others! Do they see Him when they look at you?

Practice The Word:
How can you shine your LIGHT today?

Study Deeper:
1 John 1:5-10, Matthew 5:14-16 & 1 Thessalonians 5:4-6.

22. GRACE

"For it is by grace you have been saved, through faith, and this is not from yourselves, it is the gift of God, not by works, so that no one can boast." Ephesians 2:8-9 (NIV)

"You then, my son, be strong in the grace that is in Christ Jesus." 2 Timothy 2:1 (NIV)

"But I do not account my life of any value nor as precious to myself, if only I may finish my course and the ministry that I received from the Lord Jesus, to testify to the gospel of the grace of God." Acts 20:24 (NIV)

✽ ✽ ✽

Grace: *unmerited divine assistance given to humans for their regeneration or sanctification, a virtue coming from God, a state of sanctification enjoyed through divine assistance.*

Grace is one of those gifts that is so undeserving and yet God offers it to you freely. You can do nothing to earn it and can't take any credit for it because Jesus bought it for you with His own blood on the cross. He's just waiting for you to receive it.

If you have already received His grace, scripture says to live strongly in it. Don't let a day go by without remembering the grace you were shown. You have the opportunity to testify of God's grace in your life to those around you. Are you taking advantage of each moment you are given? It could be the way you live in God's grace that draws someone else to receive His free gift today.

Practice The Word:
Who can you show GRACE to today?

Study Deeper:
Ephesians 2:1-10, 2 Timothy 1:8-14 & Romans 3:23-26 & 5:15-21.

23. PURPOSE

"For in him all things were created: things in heaven and on earth, visible and invisible, whether thrones or powers or rulers or authorities; all things have been created through him and for him." Colossians 1:16 (NIV)

"And we know that in all things God works for the good of those who love him, who have been called according to his purpose." Romans 8:28 (NIV)

"But you are a chosen people, a royal priesthood, a holy nation, God's special possession, that you may declare the praises of him who called you out of darkness into his wonderful light." 1 Peter 2:9 (NIV)

✾ ✾ ✾

Purpose: *the reason for which something is done or created or for which something exists.*

More and more in the world today, you hear people asking the question, what is my purpose? What was I created for? The Bible has the answer to this long asked question.

You were created on purpose, for a purpose. You were created for God. God longs to have a personal relationship with you. He wants you to enjoy His presence. God wasn't lonely that he needed to create you. He did it for His own enjoyment and pleasure. You were created to bring honor and glory to Him.

As a child of God, no matter what you are facing in life, remember that God has a purpose for you and for all that happens to you. He allows certain things for a reason and promises to work them for good for those who love Him. Do you trust Him?

The last verse, 1 Peter 2:9 says, that as God's people, *you were called out of darkness into His light so that you could declare His praises.* When you glorify God, you are fulfilling the purpose you were created for.

Practice The Word:
How can you live a life of PURPOSE today?

Study Deeper:
1 Chronicles 16:8-36, Isaiah 43:7 & Philippians 2:13-16.

24. VICTORY

"What, then, shall we say in response to these things? If God is for us, who can be against us? He who did not spare his own Son, but gave him up for us all—how will he not also, along with him, graciously give us all things? Who will bring any charge against those whom God has chosen? It is God who justifies. Who then is the one who condemns? No one. Christ Jesus who died—more than that, who was raised to life—is at the right hand of God and is also interceding for us. Who shall separate us from the love of Christ? Shall trouble or hardship or persecution or famine or nakedness or danger or sword? As it is written: 'For your sake we face death all day long; we are considered as sheep to be slaughtered.' No, in all these things we are more than conquerors through him who loved us. For I am convinced that neither death nor life, neither angels nor demons, neither the present nor the future, nor any powers, neither height nor depth, nor anything else in all creation, will be able to separate us from the love of God that is in Christ Jesus our Lord." Romans 8:31-39 (NIV)

✼ ✼ ✼

Victory: *the overcoming of an enemy or antagonist, achievement of mastery or success in a struggle or endeavor against odds or difficulties.*

As Paul penned these words to the church in Rome, he spoke bold truth over their life. He encouraged them not to be overcome by their circumstances, but rather, live in the victory that Jesus offers thru His death and resurrection.

How about you? No matter what you are struggling with or the situations that arise in your life, are you ready and willing to choose victory over them? You have the power to conquer and overcome them given to you thru Jesus. Choosing to live the victorious life daily could be your greatest testimony yet.

Practice The Word:
In what area of your life can you choose VICTORY today?

Study Deeper:
Romans 8.

25. PEACE

"Peace I leave with you; my peace I give you. I do not give to you as the world gives. Do not let your hearts be troubled and do not be afraid." John 14:27 (NIV)

"I have told you these things, so that in me you may have peace. In this world you will have trouble. But take heart! I have overcome the world." John 16:33 (NIV)

❊ ❊ ❊

Peace: *totality or completeness, success, fulfillment, wholeness, harmony, security and well-being.*

Peace is not felt by most these days, but it is longed for and desired. The world tries to find peace in all the wrong places. True Peace is found only in Jesus.

As Jesus was preparing to leave this earth, He told His disciples that besides the gift of the Holy Spirit, He was also leaving them His peace. He tells us not to be troubled or afraid, rest in Him, knowing that He has overcome the world. What an incredible assurance that gives us.

A command is given in Philippians 4:6-7, but followed with a reward. *"Do not be anxious about anything (command), but in every situation, by prayer and petition, with thanksgiving, present your requests to God. And the peace of God (reward), which transcends all understanding, will guard your hearts and your minds in Christ Jesus."*

Practice The Word:
What are you worrying about that you need to lay at Jesus feet and choose His PEACE today?

Study Deeper:
Colossians 3:1-17 & Isaiah 26:3.

26. KINDNESS

"But the fruit of the Spirit is love, joy, peace, patience, kindness, goodness, faithfulness, gentleness, self-control; against such things there is no law. Now those who belong to Christ Jesus have crucified the flesh with its passions and desires. If we live by the Spirit, let us also walk by the Spirit." Galatians 5:22-25 (NASB)

"Do not let kindness and truth leave you; Bind them around your neck, Write them on the tablet of your heart." Proverbs 3:3 (NASB)

❈ ❈ ❈

Kindness: *the quality of being friendly, generous, and considerate.*

Jesus lived out this virtue to the fullest during His 33 years of life on this earth. He showed the definition of kindness to those around Him daily.

Kindness is an important virtue because it is one of the ways in which others will know you are a child of God. It is a fruit that should be evident in every believers life. If kindness is seen in you, it is confirmation that the Holy Spirit is at work in your life making you more like Jesus.

King Solomon said it well when he said to, *bind it around your neck and write it on the tablet of your heart.* In other words, it should be permanently seen.

Jesus is your example again when it comes to showing kindness. Remember, don't just show it to the ones who are easy, let it be shown even greater to the ones who are difficult in your life. Think of the kindness Jesus showed you on the cross.

Practice The Word:
Who can you show KINDNESS to today?

Study Deeper:
Titus 3:4-7, Isaiah 54:10 & Psalm 63.

27. ABIDING

"I am the true vine, and my Father is the vinedresser. Every branch in me that does not bear fruit he takes away, and every branch that does bear fruit he prunes, that it may bear more fruit. Already you are clean because of the word that I have spoken to you. Abide in me, and I in you. As the branch cannot bear fruit by itself, unless it abides in the vine, neither can you, unless you abide in me. I am the vine; you are the branches. Whoever abides in me and I in him, he it is that bears much fruit, for apart from me you can do nothing. If anyone does not abide in me he is thrown away like a branch and withers; and the branches are gathered, thrown into the fire, and burned. If you abide in me, and my words abide in you, ask whatever you wish, and it will be done for you. By this my Father is glorified, that you bear much fruit and so prove to be my disciples. As the Father has loved me, so have I loved you. Abide in my love. If you keep my commandments, you will abide in my love, just as I have kept my Father's commandments and abide in his love. These things I have spoken to you, that my joy may be in you, and that your joy may be full." John 15:1-11 (ESV)

❋ ❋ ❋

Abiding: *enduring, steadfast, lasting for a long time, remain and wait.*

Abiding is a choice. Recognizing who God is (the vinedresser), who Jesus is (the vine) and who you are (the branch) is key to understanding this passage.

The vinedresser (God) takes away the branches that are not bearing fruit, but the ones that are bearing fruit He prunes. Don't be scared of the pruning process. John Trapp said, *"And if it be painful to bleed, it is worse to wither. Better be pruned to grow than cut up to burn."*

Is it your desire to be a healthy, thriving branch, connected to the vine? Remember, the purpose of the branch is to bear fruit.

The vine and branch picture stress the need for complete dependence and constant connection. Lastly, in verse 11 you see the fruit of the Spirit (joy) start to show up in the life of a believer who chooses to abide in Him. Brothers and sisters, abiding in Jesus is the only way you can bear fruit.

Practice The Word:
Choose to ABIDE in Jesus today?

Study Deeper:
John 15.

28. HONOR

"Wisdom's instruction is to fear the Lord, and humility comes before honor." Proverbs 15:33 (NIV)

"Pride brings a person low, but the lowly in spirit gain honor." Proverbs 29:23 (NIV)

"Be devoted to one another in love. Honor one another above yourselves." Romans 12:10 (NIV)

❋ ❋ ❋

Honor: *high respect; great esteem.*

I will never forget one of the first things my husband said to me when we started dating, he wanted to honor me as his sister in Christ. It caught me off guard a little, but as time went on I saw him (and still do) living out that word towards me. That meant more than I can put into words.

Brothers and sisters, what a rich word you get to practice. But, what does honor look like? In the first 2 verses above you see that humility has to come first. You have to humble yourself before God and others in order to honor those around you.

How different would you look and act if you showed real, genuine honor? Would you put others before yourself? Would you look out for others interests before your own?

It's easy to honor those we like, but not so much when it comes to those who are difficult. That is the real test of honor. Jesus called you to live a life against the normal. Remember, He is your example. He honored His Father thru His humble life here on earth and because of that He was exalted. You get to reflect Jesus in this way.

Practice The Word:
Who can you HONOR today?

Study Deeper:
Proverbs 21:21 & John 12:20-26.

29. THANKFULNESS

"Let the peace of Christ rule in your hearts, to which indeed you were called in one body; and be thankful. Let the word of Christ richly dwell within you, with all wisdom teaching and admonishing one another with psalms and hymns and spiritual songs, singing with thankfulness in your hearts to God." Colossians 3:15-16 (NASB)

"Give thanks to the Lord, for he is good; his love endures forever." 1 Chronicles 16:34 (NIV)

"I will give thanks to you, Lord, with all my heart; I will tell of all your wonderful deeds." Psalm 9:1 (NIV)

* * *

Thankfulness: *feeling or expressing gratitude; appreciative.*

Learning to cultivate a heart of thankfulness is crucial for the life of a believer. There is *always* something you can be thankful for. When your life seems to be spinning out of control, take a step back and remember you can thank God that even then, He is Sovereign and in control.

How do you develop a thankful heart? I believe that the more you spend time in the truth of God's Word, your response will be of overflowing gratitude to God for all He's done. Often, as you can see in the verses above, thankfulness leads to singing your praises to God. The Psalms are full of thankful songs.

Thankfulness is one of those virtues that can be contagious. Often the word contagious is not a positive word, but in this sense it is. When I've been around people who are genuinely thankful, it causes me to stop and think of all the ways God has blessed my life. Do people see you with a heart of thankfulness?

Practice The Word:
What are you THANKFUL for today?

Study Deeper:
Psalm 69:30, 92 & 95.

30. GROWTH

"Therefore, dear friends, since you have been forewarned, be on your guard so that you may not be carried away by the error of the lawless and fall from your secure position. But grow in the grace and knowledge of our Lord and Savior Jesus Christ. To Him be glory both now and forever! Amen." 2 Peter 3:17-18 (NIV)

"Therefore let us move beyond the elementary teachings about Christ and be taken forward to maturity..." Hebrews 6:1a (NIV)

❋ ❋ ❋

Growth: *the process of increasing and developing.*

As a parent one of our main goals is to encourage our child to grow. We don't want them to stay a baby their whole life. We feed them healthy food, play to get exercise and help them develop good sleeping habits. This is all part of good physical growth.

Move that concept over to your spiritual growth. Your heavenly Father has the same desires for you to grow spiritually in your relationship with Him. Don't be satisfied to be a spiritual baby or child your whole life, push yourself to grow in His grace and knowledge. He longs to take you deeper. In Luke 2:52 it says that, *"Jesus grew in wisdom and stature, and in favor with God and man."* Even Jesus knew the importance of spiritual growth. He is your example.

Practice The Word:
How can you GROW in your walk with God today?

Study Deeper:
2 Peter.

NOTES

- Bible NASB (New American Standard Bible), ESV (English Standard Version), NIV (New International Version)
- Cambridge Dictionary
- Oxford Dictionary
- Spurgeon, Charles Haddon The New Park Street Pulpit, Volumes 1-6 and The Metropolitan Tabernacle Pulpit, Volumes 7-63 (Pasadena, Texas: Pilgrim Publications, 1990)
- Trapp, John A Commentary on the Old and New Testaments, Volume One (Eureka, California: Tanski Publications, 1997)
- Warren, Kay Choose Joy: Because Happiness Isn't Enough
- Webster, Merriam Dictionary